SOUTH AFRICA
THE PEOPLE

Domini Clark

A Bobbie Kalman Book

The Lands, Peoples, and Cultures Series

Crabtree Publishing Company
www.crabtreebooks.com

The Lands, Peoples, and Cultures Series
Created by Bobbie Kalman

Author: Domini Clark

Revised edition: Plan B Book Packagers

Coordinating editor: Ellen Rodger

Copy editor: Adrianna Morganelli

Proofreader: Crystal Sikkens

Project editor: Robert Walker

Production coordinator: Katherine Kantor

Project development: First Folio Resource Group, Inc.
Pauline Beggs
Tom Dart
Kathryn Lane
Debbie Smith
Tara Steele
Robyn Craig

Design: David Vereschagin/Quadrat Communications

Consultants
Leon Jordan and Claudina Ramosepele, South African High Commission; Dr. Joseph R. Manyoni, Department of Sociology and Anthropology, Carleton University; Tshepoeng Mohohlo, Principal, Uitspandoorns Farm School; Professor T. Sono, Professor Extraordinary, Graduate School of Management, University of Pretoria and President, South African Institute of Race Relations; Michael Titlestad, University of South Africa

Photographs
AP/Wide World Photos: p. 15 (bottom); Archive Photos: p. 7 (bottom), 9 (bottom); John F. Burns/New York Times Co./Archive Photos: p. 14 (left); Camera Press Ltd./Archive Photos: p. 10 (left); Corbis/Charles O'Rear: p. 3; Dhoxax/Shutterstock Inc.: p. 21 (top); Jillian Edelstein/Link: p. 15 (top left); Chad Ehlers/International Stock Photo: p. 16; Orde Eliason/Link: title page, p. 4 (left); Express Newspapers/Archive Photos: p. 9 (top), 11 (bottom); Tom and Michele Grimm/International Stock Photo: p. 18 (bottom); Jan Halaska/Photo Researchers: p. 22 (top); George Holton/Photo Researchers: p. 22 (bottom); Hubertus Kanus/Photo Researchers: p. 23 (top); Rhonda Klevansky/Impact: p. 24; Jason Lauré: p. 8, 10 (right), 12 (bottom), 20 (right), 21 (bottom); Lauré Communications: p. 12 (top); Richard T. Nowitz: p. 23 (bottom); M. Timothy O'Keefe/International Stock Photo: p. 18 (top), 19 (top); Caroline Penn/Impact: p. 5 (bottom); PhotoSky 4t com/Shutterstock Inc.: p. 5 (top), 20 (bottom), 30; Porterfield/Chickering/Photo Researchers: p. 29 (bottom); Herman Potgieter/Link: p. 31; Carl Purcell: p. 19 (bottom); John Reader, Science Source/Photo Researchers: p. 6; Reuters/Mike Hutchings/Archive Photos: p. 13 (bottom); Reuters/Juda Ngwenya/Archive Photos: p. 11 (top), 15 (right); Reuters/Phillipe Wojazer/Archive Photos: p. 13 (top); Philip Schedler/Link: p. 4 (left); Vishal Shah/Shutterstock Inc.: cover; South Africa Tourism Board: p. 27 (bottom); Michael Titlestad: p. 25 (bottom); Cyril Toker/Photo Researchers: p. 7 (top); Tropix/A. Mountain: p. 17 (top and middle), 25 (top), 28; University of Cape Town: p. 14 (right); Paul Weinberg: p. 27 (top); Ingrid Mårn Wood: p. 26 (bottom), 29 (top), 30 (top)

Illustrations
Marie Lafrance: icon
David Wysotski, Allure Illustrations: back cover

Cover: A market stall owner poses with some the traditional fabrics she sells to tourists in South Africa.

Title page: Boys play a sandy game of soccer on a crowded beach.

Icon: South Africa's flag appears at the top of each section.

Back cover: The springbok is South Africa's national symbol.

Library and Archives Canada Cataloguing in Publication

Clark, Domini, 1979-
    South Africa : the people / Domini Clark. -- Rev. ed.

(The lands, peoples, and cultures series)
Includes index.
ISBN 978-0-7787-9291-8 (bound).--ISBN 978-0-7787-9659-6 (pbk.)

    1. South Africa--Social conditions--Juvenile literature. I. Title.
II. Series: Lands, peoples, and cultures series

HN801.A8C53 2008   j968   C2008-902627-6

Library of Congress Cataloging-in-Publication Data

Clark, Domini, 1979-
    South Africa. The people / Domini Clark. -- Rev. ed.
        p. cm. -- (The lands, peoples, and cultures series)
    "A Bobbie Kalman Book."
    Includes index.
    ISBN-13: 978-0-7787-9659-6 (pbk. : alk. paper)
    ISBN-10: 0-7787-9659-0 (pbk. : alk. paper)
    ISBN-13: 978-0-7787-9291-8 (reinforced library binding : alk. paper)
    ISBN-10: 0-7787-9291-9 (reinforced library binding : alk. paper)
    1. South Africa--Social life and customs--Juvenile literature. 2. Apartheid--South Africa--History--Juvenile literature. I. Title. II. Series.
DT1752.C58 2008
968--dc22
                                                        2008017485

Crabtree Publishing Company

www.crabtreebooks.com   1-800-387-7650

Published in Canada
Crabtree Publishing
616 Welland Ave.
St. Catharines, ON
L2M 5V6

Published in the United States
Crabtree Publishing
PMB16A
350 Fifth Ave., Suite 3308
New York, NY 10118

Published in the United Kingdom
Crabtree Publishing
White Cross Mills
High Town, Lancaster
LA1 4XS

Published in Australia
Crabtree Publishing
386 Mt. Alexander Rd.
Ascot Vale (Melbourne)
VIC 3032

Contents

⚑ A diverse people ⚑

Over 47 million people of many different backgrounds live in South Africa. It is a country that has throughout its history endured wars, race struggles, and more recently, severe health crises. South Africans have learned to survive and thrive despite adversity.

The struggle for equality

For many years, some South Africans were treated much better than others, depending on their **race**. This inequality led to violence and hatred. Today, South Africa is a model for racial **reconciliation**. The people of South Africa have worked hard to move beyond their troubled past, learn from one another, and to appreciate their country's diversity. This spirit of understanding has strengthened the country and the people who live there.

(above) A woman combs the tangles out of her daughter's hair.

(left) A South African of Indian background poses in front of a colorful mural.

4

(above) For years, government policies meant that white people had greater privileges in South Africa. Today, all races are working together to make the country a better place to live.

Muslims in the Malay quarter of Cape Town chat on their front doorstep.

In the 1900s, the **fossilized** skull of an infant *Australopithecus africanus*, called the Taung baby, was found in South Africa. **Anthropologists** who studied this skull, which was over two million years old, discovered that the Taung baby's teeth and brain were similar to a human's. Since then, anthropologists have found many remains of **primates** with human-like features in the country. These primates lived before the time of *homo sapiens*, or modern humans.

Hunters and gatherers

The first *homo sapiens* who lived in South Africa were the San and the Khoikhoi. Twenty thousand years ago, the San came to South Africa from other parts of the African continent. They were **nomads** who moved from place to place hunting animals and gathering plants for food. The Khoikhoi hunted and gathered too, but they also herded animals and stayed in one place for longer periods of time.

The arrival of the Bantu speakers

About 1,500 years ago, Bantu-speaking peoples from further north on the continent came to the eastern part of South Africa with their cattle. They set up villages and farms, forcing the San and Khoikhoi to move to less **fertile** land in the west. Many of the peoples who live in South Africa today, such as the Zulu, Sotho, Tswana, Ndebele, and Xhosa, are **descendants** of the Bantu-speaking peoples.

A trader's stopover

About 500 years ago, European traders and explorers sailing to and from Asia for spices docked their boats at the Cape of Good Hope in southwestern South Africa. Here, they stocked up on fresh food and water, sometimes trading with the local people. In 1652, the Dutch sent 100 people to the Cape to settle permanently. The settlers, who called themselves Boers, the Dutch word for farmers, supplied European traders with food. As more sailors used the trading base, the Dutch brought slaves from Southeast Asia to work for them. Over time, people from France and Germany joined the Boers. These people became known as Afrikaners. Their farms expanded into the lands of the Khoikhoi. Some Khoikhoi worked for the Afrikaners, while others were forced to move north.

Skulls found in South African caves are from humans' oldest ancestors. These skulls are 1.6 to 3.7 million years old!

A British colony

In the early 1800s, the Cape became part of the British **Empire**. A few thousand English people moved to the new **colony**. Some became farmers, hiring workers from India. Others set up businesses and settled in towns and cities such as East London, Durban, Port Elizabeth, and Grahamstown.

The Great Trek

The Afrikaners were not happy under British rule. In the 1830s, over 1,600 Boers left their farms and made the difficult journey inland. They fought with many African peoples, including the Khoikhoi and the Ndebele, taking over their lands and forcing them to work on the Boers' farms.

(right) Many San still live in the Kalahari Desert, where they practice many of their ancient traditions.

(below) This picture shows a wagon train of Boers, called Voortrekkers, making the trek inland.

Actors recreate the Zulu victory over the British at the Battle of Isandhlwana in this scene from a movie. By the end of the Zulu Wars later that year, the British defeated the Zulu kingdom.

The Zulu

During the 1800s, the Zulu became a powerful people. Under their leader Shaka, they became skilled warriors who fought many other African peoples and took over their lands. Some people fled before the Zulu warriors arrived. Many others were killed or captured as slaves. The Zulu also fought many wars against the Afrikaners and the British. They were eventually defeated by the British in 1879.

Diamonds, gold, and war

Diamonds were discovered in South Africa in 1867. Two decades later, gold was also found. The British, many of whom came to South Africa hoping to make their fortune, tried to take over the lands where Afrikaners had built their farms. This land had diamonds and gold located on it. War broke out between the British and the Afrikaners. Many black South Africans, who were working in the mines, were pulled into the battle on both sides. The Boer War lasted three years. After thousands of people died at the hands of the British, the Afrikaners finally **surrendered**. In 1902, all of South Africa became part of the British Empire.

Reconciliation Day

In 1838, Zulu warriors and Afrikaners fought at the Battle of Blood River. Four thousand Zulu were killed, but not a single Afrikaner died in battle. That battle is remembered every year with a holiday on December 16. The holiday used to be called the Day of the Vow because the Afrikaners vowed to God that they would honor the day if he saved them from the Zulu. The holiday is now called Reconciliation Day and is celebrated by all South Africans. It is an important holiday because it was established to **reconcile** people from different racial backgrounds and develop positive relationships after so many years of fighting.

The building of a nation for whites

Britain granted South Africa independence in 1909. In 1910, the country became a separate nation, called the Union of South Africa. Only whites could vote in the country's first elections. They chose General Louis Botha, an Afrikaner, as their prime minister. Botha passed many new laws that **discriminated** against people because of their race. For example, good jobs were reserved for white people, and no blacks were allowed in the army. In 1948, the National Party came into power. This political party, which was run by Afrikaners, stayed in power almost continually until 1994.

In 1890, the British millionaire Cecil Rhodes became prime minister of the Cape Colony. He made his fortune from mining.

Laboring in the diamond mines was very dangerous. Black workers were treated brutally by their white bosses and many died in cave-ins.

The years of apartheid

The conflict between the people of South Africa worsened in 1948, when the National Party instituted **apartheid**. Apartheid means "separateness" in Afrikaans, the language of the Afrikaners. Under apartheid, everyone in South Africa was classified as one of four **ethnic groups**: white, Indian, colored, or black. Each group had different rights. People were told what kind of work they could do and where they could live. They were not allowed to marry someone from another group. The whites, who were mostly Afrikaners and British South Africans, gave themselves the most rights to make sure that they would always be in power. Only they could vote and run for government office.

Coloreds and Indians

The word "coloreds" was used in South Africa to describe people of mixed race. Some were descendants of Dutch men and the African women who they married. Others were the descendants of San and Khoikhoi who married one another. Malays, whose **ancestors** were slaves brought by the Dutch from Southeast Asia, were also considered coloreds.

Some Indians were brought to South Africa by the British in the 1800s to work on sugar **plantations**. Wealthier Indians came as traders. Coloreds and Indians were given similar rights under apartheid. They had fewer rights than whites, but more rights than the black population.

(left) Many public areas were divided into separate areas for each race.

(below) Under apartheid, the police often used violence to enforce laws.

A man presents his pass book. Before the laws changed, black people had to show their pass books to authorities on demand.

At a demonstration during the 1950s, protesters burn their pass books. They deliberately broke the law and risked arrest.

Blacks

Apartheid was most unfair to black people. For each black ethnic group, such as the Xhosa, Zulu, or Ndebele, the government set aside an area called a **homeland**. Blacks were forced to move to their people's **designated** homeland, even though they may never have seen the place before. For them, home was back in the cities with their friends and families.

Life in these homelands was very difficult. The government gave only 13 percent of the land to 75 percent of the population. Conditions were crowded, and there was not enough housing. The soil in the homelands was poor, since most of the fertile land was given to whites, and crops often failed.

Black workers

Some black people worked on farms owned by whites just outside their homelands, but most men had to leave their families to work in the cities and mines. There, they were paid very little and often could not visit their families more than once or twice a year. They lived in **townships**, which were built for them outside of cities. The townships were crowded and there was no running water or electricity. Life in the townships was just as difficult as life in the homelands.

The Acts and the pass law

Under apartheid, the government passed acts to restrict the freedoms of non-whites. The Reservation of Separate Amenities Act ordered that all public places such as parks, toilets, buses, and swimming pools have separate sections for people of different races. The Bantu Education Act said that black children should be encouraged to do **manual labor** instead of higher-paid skilled work that was reserved for white people. One aspect of apartheid that was particularly harsh was the pass law. The law stated that all blacks had to carry identification, in the form of pass books, everywhere they went. Pass books were a way to control black people's movement: they were not allowed to visit white areas without permission. About one million black people were arrested every year for disobeying the pass law.

(above) Demonstrators flee a tear gas attack during the struggle against apartheid. Tear gas, which causes blinding tears, is used to control crowds.

Resistance

Many people were very angry about the injustices of apartheid. They resisted in whatever ways they could. There were frequent demonstrations against the government, which often responded with violence. During apartheid, many protesters were killed. Others, including many children, were jailed for long periods of time.

(above) A boy takes part in Freedom Day celebrations. Every year, on April 27, South Africans celebrate the anniversary of the first elections since the end of apartheid.

The end of apartheid

After years of protests and violence in South Africa, and growing opposition to apartheid around the world, South African president F. W. de Klerk announced the end of apartheid. In 1992, the government repealed the last of the apartheid laws. In 1994, South Africa had its first elections where everyone, no matter what their color, could vote. South Africans were not the only ones to celebrate the end of apartheid. People all over the world cheered and danced in the streets when they heard that the years of "separateness" were finally over. It would still take a long time for the wounds of apartheid to heal.

Sharpeville Massacre

On March 21, 1960, black people across South Africa protested the pass laws. In Sharpeville, a black township near Johannesburg, a crowd gathered in front of a police station to burn their pass books. The police fired on the crowd, killing 69 black people and injuring more than 180 others. After this event, many other countries started to show their disapproval of apartheid. They put pressure on the South African government by supporting anti-apartheid organizations and refusing to trade with the country. Despite this pressure, the government did not change the pass laws until 1986.

Heroes in a difficult time

The end of apartheid did not come easily. Thousands of people lost their lives in the fight for freedom. Others spent years in South African prisons or in **exile**. Among these people were leaders who organized political groups and encouraged people to stand up for themselves. These heroes are recognized worldwide as people who fought for human rights.

Nelson Mandela

Nelson Mandela is known as one of the greatest fighters for equality. Early in his career as a lawyer, Mandela worked on many cases involving black people who broke pass laws. He joined the African National Congress (ANC), a political party formed by people of all races who were against apartheid. He gave speeches, organized protests, and wrote articles criticizing the government. The government ordered Mandela several times to stop his activities. In 1963, he was sentenced to life in prison. For 27 years, people in South Africa and around the world called for Mandela to be set free. In 1990, President de Klerk finally released Mandela. The two shared the Nobel Peace Prize in 1993 for their work to end apartheid. In 1994, Mandela became South Africa's president, a position he held until he retired in 1999. In retirement, Mandela became an international icon.

Desmond Tutu

When Desmond Tutu became **archbishop** of South Africa's Anglican Church, he was put in a unique position. In a country where anti-apartheid leaders were arrested for speaking out against the government, Tutu could still voice his opinions. The government did not want to anger the church by putting such an important person in jail. Tutu opposed apartheid and the violence being used in the fight against apartheid. In 1984, he was awarded the Nobel Peace Prize for his nonviolent stand against racism.

Nelson Mandela casts a ballot at the first free elections in South Africa in 1994. Mandela became the country's first black president.

Desmond Tutu dances for joy after voting in the 1994 election. Tutu went on to be head of South Africa's Truth and Reconciliation Commission, which helped heal the wounds of apartheid.

# Country life

For most of South Africa's history, the majority of the people lived in the countryside. Black people lived in villages scattered in rural areas, while white people usually owned large farms.

The village community

Black people used to live in villages with people they were related to by blood or by marriage. A village could have as few as 50 people, or as many as 1,000. The people in the village had small plots of land where they grew some crops for themselves and other crops, such as maize and vegetables, for cash. Villages were usually organized around a central square, with an outdoor market where people could buy everything from pottery and fabric to vegetables and animals.

South Africa is famous for its vineyards and wineries, which employ many farm workers.

Then...

Life was not easy in villages. Everyone had a job to do. Men tended **livestock**, plowed fields, and built and repaired the homes. Women planted and harvested the crops by hand, did household chores, and took care of the children. Young children carried water, helped their parents in the fields, and took care of the animals. Older girls looked after their younger brothers and sisters. Older boys learned about village business and politics from the men.

...and now

Life in a village is still difficult. Today's villages have a few small shops, a school, a post office, or a courthouse, but there is often no running water, electricity, or **sewage** disposal. There are not enough doctors, and good health care is often unavailable. Most of the land is not suitable for growing crops. Many people work outside their villages. Some travel for hours to work in a town or city. Others, who work in sugar plantations or in the country's gold and diamond mines, are gone for months at a time. Many move to the city, sending money home when they can.

A villager builds the walls of her house with mud. Village homes are made from traditional materials, including mud, grasses, and wood.

Learning new ways

People who stay in their villages are finding new ways to make a living. Women often do the work that men who left the village used to do. They also teach each other new skills, such as crocheting, making school uniforms, and fixing bikes. Men who stay in the village may make crafts to sell in markets, or build bridges and roads. Some traditional villages have disappeared altogether while others have grown into modern towns.

(below) Villagers wait their turn at the central water pump. Many villages do not have running water and some have only recently been wired for electricity.

Farm settlements

Large, modern farms are found throughout South Africa. Farm workers use tractors and other up-to-date farming equipment to make harvesting the crops easier and faster. Farm workers and their families sometimes live in settlements nearby. Families typically live in two-room cement houses with corrugated iron roofs. A number of **migrant** workers, who travel from farm to farm to help with the harvest, sleep in one large building. There is no electricity or running water, so meals are cooked over open fires and water comes from a pump outside. Sometimes there is medical care, and some settlements have schools with good teachers but little in the way of extras such as library books and computers.

#

Until the late 1800s, Zulu people lived with members of their extended family in small groups scattered across the countryside. Each settlement was called a *kraal* in Afrikaans, or an *umuzi* in *isiZulu*, the language of the Zulu people.

The *umuzi*

The *umuzi* was a circular group of beehive-shaped huts that was often surrounded by a fence. According to Zulu custom, a man could have more than one wife at a time. Each wife lived in her own hut, called an *indlu*, with her children. All the children in the *umuzi* were considered brothers and sisters, and all of the father's wives were considered their mothers.

Life at the *umuzi*

At the center of the *umuzi* was a cattle pen where the valuable livestock were kept at night. Cattle were so important in Zulu life that there were over 100 words in *isiZulu* to describe their color. Men tended the cattle. Women were not allowed near the animals because it was believed they might **contaminate** them. Women raised the children, kept the huts clean, and looked after crops such as sorghum, maize, sweet potatoes, and cocoa-yams. As the crops grew, the young boys of the *umuzi* stood on special platforms to scare away birds and animals that ate the crops. Once the crops were harvested, they were stored in huts high above the ground, away from the animals, or in pits in the ground.

Having fun

Young children often played games such as tag. Older boys played games that would make them better hunters. In one game, a boy rolled a soft fruit or vegetable down a steep hill. The boys at the bottom of the hill threw their spears at it. Whoever speared the moving target was the next to roll the fruit or vegetable down the hill.

(above) Some Zulu work at cultural centers that recreate their traditional ways of life for tourists. These men are cooking a meal.

(right) A spearmaker at a cultural center checks his work.

Zulu women at a cultural center wear traditional dress including wide, red hats.

Changing times

Traditional Zulu life changed in the late 1800s when the British gave much of the Zulu's good farmland to white people. Zulu life changed again in the early 1900s when the British introduced taxation. Before taxation, the Zulu raised just enough livestock and crops to feed themselves. After taxation, they had to earn money to pay taxes. They opened stores where they sold their crafts and vegetables, went to work on Afrikaners' farms, and moved to the cities and mines to find work.

Today, few Zulu live in an *umuzi*. Most live in cities and work at a variety of jobs. Visitors can still see the traditional Zulu lifestyle in parts of South Africa. Special villages have been built where tourists can stay overnight in traditional Zulu huts, watch Zulu dances, learn about Zulu fighting techniques, and eat Zulu foods.

*A man peers out of the low door of a beehive hut. The doorway to the **indlu** is low so that people have to bow down as they enter, paying respect to the elders.*

19

⚐ The big city ⚐

Today, more than half of South Africa's population lives in cities and towns. Some cities, such as Cape Town and Durban, grew from small trading posts and port towns. Others, such as Johannesburg, sprung up as people moved to the area to work in gold and diamond mines.

A bustling scene

South African cities are centers of business, government, and entertainment. Early in the morning, buses and trains packed with commuters head downtown. People rush to their jobs in high-rise office buildings that house the headquarters of huge companies. Some work in supermarkets, clothing factories, or hotels. Others are university professors, doctors, business executives, or lawyers.

(above) From Table Mountain, above Cape Town, you can see the houses, roads, and businesses of Cape Town spread out below.

(right) A vendor sells fruit on a street in Johannesburg.

Daily grind

At lunch, people crowd the streets again, grabbing *boerewors*, a type of sausage, from a street vendor or visiting the downtown markets. You can hear different languages as people chat to one another during their midday break. At the end of the day, many people crowd back on the buses and trains for their return trip home. Others stay downtown to wander through bookstores, libraries, and museums, to have dinner at a restaurant, or to go to the theater.

Life in the cities and suburbs

White people have always lived in the cities and in the wealthy **suburbs**. Before apartheid, people from other ethnic groups lived in the cities too. They were forced to move from their neighborhoods when apartheid began. Today, people from many backgrounds are returning to the cities to look for homes and work. Usually, each group lives in its own neighborhood, although people are now free to live wherever they choose. Most homes in the city have electricity, telephones, and clean water. Some also have pools, satellite dishes, and big screen televisions.

Life in the townships

Life is quite different in the townships, where the majority of black people still live. While many families live in comfortable homes, some live in cramped, one-room buildings. Unemployment is a big problem, although some people are creating work for themselves. Men drive taxis or buses, or they set up *spaza* shops where they sell household goods and groceries. Women make crafts and clothes, prepare and sell their own food, or work as hairdressers or housekeepers in the city.

(above) Township houses are often far different than houses in other South African cities and suburbs.

(below) Khayalitsha is a township north of Cape Town. Many people moved here to find work in Cape Town, despite the long trip to the city.

The type of home that people live in depends on where they live. Most people in the city live in high-rise apartment buildings or in ordinary brick or cement houses. People in the townships often live in smaller homes, and some villagers live in round huts.

One-room homes

Owning a home is very expensive for many people in the townships. Often, people live in a one-room house built in a relative's backyard. As more and more people look for work in the city, the townships are becoming even more crowded with people settling there. Many people build huts for themselves using whatever material is available: cardboard, scrap wood, metal sheets, even tin cans and soda bottles. These homes can be jammed so close together that it is difficult to walk between them.

(above) This couple built their home out of corrugated metal, a fairly sturdy material.

The Ndebele people often paint their houses with bright geometric patterns.

Rondavels

Some people in South Africa's rural areas live in traditional round huts called rondavels. The Zulu make their beehive huts by tying branches together in the shape of a dome, placing the branches in the ground, then laying tightly woven grasses on top. Other rondavels, such as the huts of the Xhosa and the Venda, have walls of tall reeds.

Cape Dutch architecture

Early Dutch settlers in Cape Town and the surrounding area developed their own style of architecture. They built white, one-story houses made of brick, plaster, or wood. The houses are usually symmetrical, which means that one side looks exactly the same as the other. Windows with shutters run in long, straight lines along the length of the building. Large doorways in the center often have huge pillars in front of them and a **gable** on top that reaches higher than the steep roof. The most elaborate homes have a *stoep*, or verandah, with seats at each end.

(above) A beehive hut's rounded shape helps keep the hut in place when strong winds blow.

(below) Cape Dutch houses, such as this farmhouse, were built by the first Dutch settlers.

In South African schools, children of all ages learn to read and write in different languages, do arithmetic problems, and discuss important topics. Children of different ethnic groups study and play together. This was not always the case.

How things have changed

During apartheid, black, white, Indian, and colored children all went to different schools. Many children could not afford to go to school at all. School was free only for white children. Today, schools are free for everyone and children of all races can go to any school. There are still many differences between schools in wealthy areas and schools in areas where people have less money.

Schools in wealthy areas and privately run schools that charge fees are located in bright buildings, with computers in every classroom, textbooks for each student, and many well-trained teachers. In other areas, especially in villages, there are not enough teachers or books to go around. Fifty students of different ages might be in one classroom and the teacher may teach several grades at a time.

In class

In black townships, children are taught in their ethnic language. For example, in a school in a Xhosa area, children would learn in *isiXhosa* until grade 5. After that, students are taught in English and learn Afrikaans as well. Many South African children speak at least three languages.

Most schools in South Africa open at 7:30 a.m. and classes are held until 2:00 p.m. The school may stay open for a few more hours after that. During this time, students can get extra help from their teacher, or do their homework if they do not have a quiet place to study at home. After school, students participate in the same kinds of activities as other students around the world: choir, chess, sports, drama, and public speaking.

Friends wearing their school uniforms play clapping games during recess.

Rural schools

In areas where public transportation is either unavailable or is too expensive, students walk to school. They must often leave their home hours before school starts to arrive on time. Children start school at different ages. Young children who live far from school cannot walk the long distance, so they stay home. Other children stay at home for a few years to help their parents with farm work. There are students as old as thirteen who are just starting school.

Farm schools

Students in rural communities often go to a school provided especially for the children of farm workers. The whole community, including the students, takes care of the school. Students are expected to sweep out the classroom and look after the grounds after class. If they are lucky, a local farmer might donate a fence for the schoolyard.

(above) In rural areas of South Africa, children start the long walk to school in the early morning. Most schools require students to wear a uniform such as a white or blue shirt and black shorts, pants, or skirts.

(below) A teacher leads a farm school choir through practice as two of its members dance to the music. Farm schools are schools for the children of rural farm workers. The schools are often basic and rely on farmers to donate land and sometimes even equipment.

South Africa's climate makes it the perfect place for outdoor activities. People like to fish, hike, surf, and swim. They fill huge stadiums to cheer on their national teams. Sports are also an important part of school life. Students run races and play team sports like basketball, which is becoming more and more popular.

Soccer

Children play soccer wherever there is an open space — in parks, in playgrounds, and on streets. In the countryside, people even clear away bushes and play barefoot. They use a soccer ball if they have one, but any round object will do.

Rugby players push against each other in a scrum. They are trying to kick the ball to a teammate standing just outside the scrum.

Rugby

Rugby is a lot like football. There are two teams. Each team tries to score by kicking or carrying an oval-shaped ball across the other team's goal line. Players move the ball from one end of the field to the other by kicking it forward or by passing it from side to side or backward. Rugby is a rough game where players tackle each other for the ball. The only protective gear they wear are shin guards and a mouth guard. At the end of the game, every player is dirty and bruised.

Cricket

The British brought cricket to South Africa. In this game, which is similar to baseball, two teams take turns batting and fielding. The batsman stands in front of a wicket, which is made of three wooden stumps with two sticks, called bails, on top. A bowler on the other team throws a ball and tries to knock a bail off. The batter tries to hit the ball with the flat side of his bat. If a bail is knocked off, the batsman is out. If the batsman hits the ball, he runs to the wicket on the other side of the field and scores a point. The player can run back and forth between the wickets, scoring points until the ball is returned.

Netball

Netball is probably the most popular South African game for schoolgirls and women. There are seven players on a team. A ball is passed between players, who must each stay in a certain area of the playing field. Players cannot run with the ball, but they can swivel from one foot to the other. The objective is to get the ball to a shooter, who then throws the ball through a hoop.

(above) Girls warm up before a game of netball.

A batsman stands ready to hit the bowler's throw.

# Puso's day

"Puso, time to wake up. Puso, get up! You are not going to make me late for work again. Besides," says Puso's mother more gently, "Wouldn't you like to be the first to wish Grandma a happy birthday?"

Puso leaps out of bed and runs out of his family's home, which is in his grandmother's backyard. He passes his Uncle Jairus's home as he races across the yard, around the side of the brick house, and up the front steps. Even though it is only 5:30 a.m., there is a light on in the kitchen. He tiptoes up to Grandma, gives her a big hug, and announces, "Happy birthday!" "Thank you, Puso. Since you're here early, why don't you take a shower?" Usually, Puso washes from a basin in his parents' home, because they do not have running water.

After his shower, Puso takes a bucket full of water back to his mother so she can make breakfast. Puso's mother lights the **kerosene** burner, puts on some water for coffee, and makes **mealies** for breakfast. She scoops some of the warm cornmeal mush into a bowl for Puso. Puso's father pulls himself out of bed with a long stretch. "Since I'm awake, I may as well join you." Puso feels a little guilty for waking up his father. He does not have to get up as early as Puso and Puso's mother, who have to catch a bus into downtown Johannesburg. Puso's father has a good construction job building houses in Soweto, where they live.

"Let's get going," says Puso's mother as she ties up her hair in a kerchief. Puso kisses his father goodbye and runs to catch up with his mother. At the bus stop, two full buses go by. They board the third bus and even get a seat.

"Johannesburg, Rotunda Bus Terminal!" the bus driver bellows after an hour or so. Puso and his mother get off the bus. "Oh, look!" says Puso's mother. "There's your friend, Inge. And there's my next bus." With a quick peck on the cheek, Puso's mother hurries across the station and greets her friends from the canning factory.

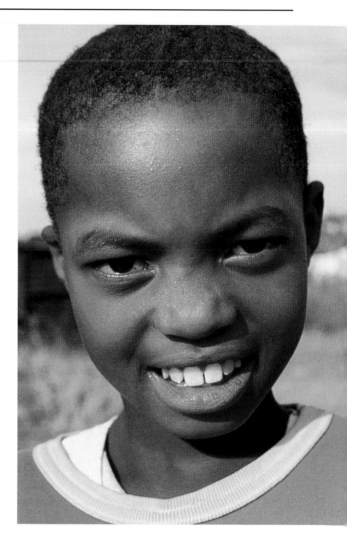

Puso is eleven years old and lives in Soweto, a part of Johannesburg where nearly 900,000 people live.

During their short walk to school, Inge and Puso have fun teaching each other their parents' language. Inge is Afrikaner and Puso is Motswana. They both know that only a few years ago, they would not have been in the same school.

Puso and Inge reach school at 7:45, just as the bell rings. This morning, Puso has geography and math classes. At lunch hour, some of his friends start a game of soccer. Puso joins in and scores a goal just before the bell rings.

Puso's mom and dad stand outside of their house in his grandma's backyard. His parents have almost saved enough money for a brick house of their own.

By 2:00, classes are done. Usually, Puso stays after school to do his homework until his mother picks him up. Today, his mother is taking a computer class after work, so he leaves earlier with his friend Thandiwe and Thandiwe's mother, Mrs. Mhlongo. Mrs. Mhlongo knows that it is a long bus ride, so she buys Puso and Thandiwe each *kota*, or bunny chow. Puso loves *kota*, with its spicy meat filling!

After Puso gets off at his stop in Soweto, he runs all the way home. He finds his father and uncle setting up the barbecue for Grandma's birthday party. Puso goes into Grandma's house to get some chairs.

Puso's relatives gather in the backyard that evening. It is very crowded but they all have fun. Puso's uncle is at the grill all evening, flipping skewers of marinated beef. By the time Puso's mother gets home, the party is winding down, and Puso is fast asleep.

The bus stop where Puso and his mom wait for the bus to Johannesburg each morning is usually very crowded.

29

The decades of apartheid still affect life in South Africa, even though apartheid no longer exists. While everyone now has equal rights, the rainbow nation, as South Africa is sometimes called, faces many challenges.

New jobs

Under apartheid, many black people could get only low-paying jobs, even if they were well-educated. To make sure that these people have better opportunities in the workplace, the government has made it illegal to refuse a job to anyone based on their race, religion, or **gender**. As well, if the government needs work done for it, such as building roads or office buildings, it tries to hire companies that have made progress in hiring people of different races. Many black people have also received pay increases, so they now earn the same as white people doing the same job. Even with access to more jobs, it will take black people many years to make up for their lack of opportunities and experience during apartheid.

(above) Friends play in the public gardens of Cape Town.

Two boys enjoy a day of sailing near Cape Town.

Living conditions

Many black people still live in unhealthy conditions. In the years since the end of apartheid, the government has spent millions of dollars to improve life in rural areas, in the townships, and in overcrowded parts of the cities. The money is being used to build new and better houses, and to provide clean water, electricity, and sewage removal. The government is giving good farmland back to black farmers and allowing farmers to borrow money so that they can buy better animals and better seeds for crops.

New challenges

South Africa is fighting a difficult battle with HIV and AIDS, diseases that kill an estimated 1,000 South Africans a day. Many of those infected are young people between the ages of 14 and 45. For years the government, busy rebuilding the country after apartheid, was slow to act. Now, money is being spent on drugs and action plans to help people with the disease live longer and to prevent other people from getting the disease. Still, there is much more to do to help South Africans suffering through this epidemic.

Boys leap excitedly into a swimming pool on a hot day.

Glossary

ancestor A person from whom one is descended

anthropologist A person who studies how humans, their customs, and their beliefs have changed over time

apartheid A policy of separating people based on their race

archbishop An important Christian religious leader, who is responsible for the religious matters of a large area known as an archdiocese

colony An area controlled by a distant country

commission A group of people who are given the authority to carry out a certain duty

contaminate To make impure

descendant A person who can trace his or her family roots to a certain family or group

designate To select and set aside

discriminate To treat unfairly because of race, religion, gender, or other factors

empire A group of countries under one ruler or government

ethnic group People who share a common language, religion, and history

exile To force a person to leave his or her country or home

fertile Able to produce abundant crops or vegetation

fossilize To turn into stone

gable A triangular section of a roof that serves as decoration over a door or window

gender Classification in terms of male or female

homeland An area that is identified with a particular people or ethnic group

kerosene A type of oil that is used as fuel

livestock Farm animals

manual labor Work done by hand

mealie Corn

migrant A person who moves from place to place looking for work

nomad A person with no fixed home who moves from place to place in search of food and shelter

pardon A legal document that frees someone from punishment

plantation A large farm on which crops such as cotton and sugar grow

primate A member of the group of mammals that includes humans, apes, and monkeys

race A group of people having a similar ancestry

reconcile To become friends again

repeal To change back officially

sewage The waste from homes and businesses that passes through sewers and drains

suburb A community on the edge of a city

surrender To give up whatever one is fighting for to the other side

township An urban area in South Africa in which black people were forced to live

 Index

Printed in the U.S.A.